Dollars in the Dust

David Walke

Stanley Thornes (Publishers) Ltd

© David Walke 1978

All rights reserved. No part of this publication may be reproduced or transmitted in any form or by any means, electronic or mechanical, including photocopy, recording, or any information storage and retrieval system, without permission in writing from the publisher or under licence from the Copyright Licensing Agency Limited. Further details of such licences (for reprographic reproduction) may be obtained from the Copyright Licensing Agency Limited, of 90 Tottenham Court Road, London W1P 9HE.

First published in 1978 by Hutchinson Education
Reprinted in 1982, 1984, 1988

Reprinted in 1991 by
Stanley Thornes (Publishers) Ltd
Old Station Drive
Leckhampton
CHELTENHAM GL53 0DN
England

ISBN 0 7487 1047 7

Cover photograph by Steve Richards
Cover design by Martin Grant-Hudson
Printed and bound in Great Britain at Martin's of Berwick

1

Sam tossed the silver dollar high into the air. It twisted and flashed in the sun. Rock drew his gun and fired. The bullet smashed into the coin and sent it spinning to the ground. Nash picked it up and held it for Sam to see. Sam turned in his wheelchair and looked at his silver dollar. There was a hole, clean through the middle of it.

Sam turned to Rock. 'You can sure handle a gun, mister,' he said. Rock said nothing. He slipped the gun back into its holster and walked slowly over to Nash. Nash flipped the dollar to him and Rock caught it. He looked at the coin and then handed it to Sam.

'And what about you, mister?' Sam said to Nash. 'Are you as fast as your partner?' Nash shook his head. 'Ain't nobody as fast as my partner,' he said. 'But I can take care of myself.' 'So show me,' said Sam.

Nash looked around him. He saw the silver dollar Sam had in his hand. 'Hold up the dollar, Sam,' said Nash. 'Hold it high, and hold it still.' Sam looked at him, trying to figure out what Nash was going to do. 'Just do it, Sam,' he said. So Sam held the dollar up.

Nash walked away from Sam. After a few steps he turned

to face him. As he turned, his hand went to the inside of his coat. There was a glint of steel as Nash brought out a knife. The blade flashed as he threw it. The knife hit the dollar and smacked it out of Sam's fingers. Sam jerked his hand back. It had all happened so fast. Sam was amazed.

'Hell, boy,' he shouted. 'I ain't never seen anything like that!' Nash smiled. 'It's a gift, Sam baby,' he said. 'And I use it.' Nash walked over and picked up his knife. 'So you've seen what we can do, Sam,' he said. 'Now will you tell us what this is all about?'

Sam looked at them both. Rock stood tall and solid. His strong arms were folded across his broad chest. Nash was shorter and much thinner. His face was tanned with the sun. His blue eyes were sharp and bright.

Sam could tell they were the men he was looking for. So he said, 'I've got a job needs doing. It'll take two men like you to do it.' 'How much?' asked Nash. 'I'll give you two hundred dollars each,' said Sam. 'Make it three hundred and you've got yourself a deal,' said Nash.

Sam thought it over for a moment. 'OK,' he said. 'Three hundred each.' 'So what's the job?' said Nash.

Sam pulled a piece of yellow paper from his pocket. He unfolded it and held it out for Nash and Rock to see.

There were lines and marks drawn on it, and it was torn down one side.

'This here is half a map,' said Sam. 'I want you to get me the other half.' Nash looked at the map, then at Sam. 'That's it?' he asked. 'Three hundred dollars each to bring you half a map? Where's the catch?'

'There's no catch, boys,' said Sam. 'Me and my partner Moss, we've got something hid. This is the map of where to find it. I've got one half, Moss has got the other. But I got word a couple of days ago that Moss had got himself into a fight. He's shot pretty bad, and he won't last out much longer. I want the other half of the map from him before he dies. He's in a place called River Bend, three days west of here. I can't go myself when I'm stuck in this wheelchair. I want you boys to go for me and get the other half of the map.'

Nash took out a cigar and lit it. 'And what have you got hid, Sam?' he asked. Sam smiled. 'Well, mister,' he said. 'You bring me the other half of this map and I just might tell you.' He pulled some bank-notes from his pocket and counted them. 'I'll give you each a hundred now,' said Sam. 'You'll get the rest when you come back with the map.' Sam handed over the money to Nash and Rock. Then he folded his half of the map and put it in his pocket.

5

'One other thing,' said Sam. 'You'll need something to show Moss that I sent you.' He took off the good-luck charm that he wore round his neck. 'Take this. It's a charm an old Indian made for me. Moss knows it's mine. He'll know that I sent you when he sees it.'

Sam handed Nash the charm. It was small, round and made of wood, and hung on a leather lace. There was a bird carved on the front of the charm. Nash tied it round his neck. 'Let's hope it brings us luck,' he said. 'I doubt it,' said Sam. 'It darn well never brought me any!'

Nash and Rock walked over to their horses and untied them. Rock mounted, Nash turned and looked across to Sam. 'So long, Sam,' he said. 'We'll see you in a few days.' 'Adios, boys,' said Sam.

Nash swung himself into the saddle. 'Let's ride, partner,' he said, and the two cowboys galloped off down the trail that led away from the ranch.

2

Rock pulled his horse up hard and the dust flew up in a cloud.

'I need a drink,' he said to Nash. The two men tied their horses to the rail. They slapped the dust from their clothes. Nash pushed the swing doors, and Rock followed him into the saloon. The shade of the saloon was cool.

'Welcome to River Bend, boys,' said the bar-tender. 'What'll it be?' 'Whisky,' said Rock. 'Two glasses, one bottle.' The whisky washed the dry dust from their lips. Nash poured himself another drink.

'We're looking for Moss,' he said to the bar-tender. 'Is he around here?' 'Are you friends of his?' asked the bar-tender. 'Friends of a friend,' said Nash. 'He's upstairs,' said the bar-tender. 'The room at the back. But he's shot bad. He won't last out much longer.'

Nash put two dollars on the bar for the whisky. Then he and Rock turned and went upstairs. Rock checked his gun.

The room at the back was at the end of a dark passage. Nash pushed the door open slowly. He and Rock went in. The stench of whisky, sweat and blood hung in the air.

Moss lay in the big brass bed. The towel hanging on the end of the bed was red with blood.

Moss slowly turned his head and looked at the two men. He said nothing at first. Then his lips began to move.

'What do you want?' he whispered. 'Sam sent us,' said Nash, and he showed Moss Sam's Indian charm which hung round his neck. 'He wants the map.'

Moss looked up at the charm and nodded. 'I figured Sam would send somebody,' he said. 'Did he tell you about it?' Nash shook his head.

'I hid the stuff . . . made a map,' said Moss slowly. 'What stuff, Moss, what have you got hid?' asked Nash.

Moss licked his dry lips. He was breathing fast. 'Whisky,' he gasped. 'Give me whisky.' 'Take it easy,' said Nash. He poured some whisky from the bottle on the table and held the glass to Moss's lips. Moss gulped it down. Then he lay back.

'What have you got hid, what is it?' asked Nash again. 'Diamonds,' whispered Moss. Nash looked at Rock, then back at Moss. 'What diamonds?' he asked. 'Where did you get them?'

Moss spoke slowly and his voice was weak. 'Me and Sam was down in Mexico. We joined up with this other guy. His name was Kelly. We were looking for an easy bank to hit. But then we came across this big ranch. It was near San Carlos. It looked a real rich place, with a big house and all.

So we broke in one night. We found a safe and busted it open. It looked like there was no money in it, just a lot of papers. Then under all the papers Sam found this box. It wasn't very big, but when we opened it, it was full of diamonds. We'd found a fortune.'

Moss stopped and closed his eyes. Nash poured him some more whisky. 'So what happened?' asked Rock.

'We took the diamonds and got out of there. Then we found a place to bed down for the night. We were going to split the diamonds three ways. But I guess Kelly got greedy. He pulled a shot-gun on Sam and me. He said he was going to take all the diamonds. Sam went for his gun, but Kelly shot him in the legs. Darn near blew them off. I grabbed the diamonds and went for my horse. Kelly came after me but I got away. I hid the diamonds and made the map.

I met up with Sam a couple of weeks later. His legs were all busted and he was in a wheel-chair. We figured Kelly would still be looking for us. So we were going to lay low for a while till things had cooled down. Then we were going to get the diamonds back. I gave Sam half the map and I kept the other half.

Moss closed his eyes. 'More whisky,' he gasped.

'This Kelly, is it Kid Kelly?' asked Nash as he poured the drink. Moss nodded, then gulped the whisky down. 'Do you know him, Nash?' asked Rock. 'I've seen him,' said Nash. 'He's mean, a killer. You gave him the slip, but he'll be after you.'

'He knows where I am, boys,' said Moss. 'And he knows about the map. I was down in the saloon a few days ago. I got drunk. I started to shout my mouth off about the diamonds and the map. I was a darn fool. I didn't know it, but there was a cowboy at the bar who rides with Kid Kelly. He heard what I was saying and tried to get the map off me.

We got into a fight and I was shot. The sheriff broke the fight up but the cowboy got away. I guess he went to find Kelly and tell him about the map. Kelly will be back for that map, and he'll come with his men. Get the map to Sam before Kelly shows up.'

'Where is the map?' asked Nash. 'Under the pillow,' said Moss. Nash felt under the pillow on the bed. He pulled out a torn bit of yellow paper. It was the other half of the map.

'I want you to take that bag too,' said Moss. There was an old leather saddle-bag on the chair by the window. The word MOSS was burned onto the front of it. Nash went over and picked it up. It felt heavy. He opened it. Inside was a gun and a watch and a couple of silver dollars.

'That's all I've got,' said Moss. 'Put the map in the bag. Take it all back to Sam. I ain't got no more use for it. I'm nearly finished, I'm shot too bad.' Nash put the map in the bag.

'Now give me some whisky,' said Moss. 'Just give me the bottle.' He suddenly cried with the pain in his body. Nash held the bottle to Moss's lips. The dying man took a mouthful. Then he looked up at Nash. 'You'd better get going,' he whispered. 'So long boys.'

His head fell to one side. Rock went to the door. As he opened it, he turned to Nash. 'What if Kelly finds Moss here?' he said.

Nash looked down at the bed, then at Rock. 'Kelly won't get much out of him,' he said, and he pulled the blood-stained sheet over Moss's staring eyes. 'He just died.'

11

3

Kid Kelly came across the desert, out of the sun. He did not ride alone. Four gun-men rode behind the tall man dressed in black. The dust rose high as they galloped.

Nash and Rock stepped out of the saloon into the heat of the day. The street was empty. A dog barked. Far away they could hear the sound of horses.

'It sure is hot,' said Rock. Nash bit the end of a cigar. 'It's going to get a lot hotter,' he said. 'How come?' said Rock.

Nash lit his cigar. The smoke curled slowly. 'I lay odds this is Kelly,' he said. Nash nodded towards the desert. Rock turned, and they watched the five riders far off. The men were riding hard. The dust rose high in a cloud behind them.

Nash dragged on his cigar. He blew the smoke out softly. Rock leaned back on the wall and felt for his gun. They watched as the men got nearer.

The sound of the horses got louder. They could see the riders clearly now. The man out in front sat tall in the saddle. His hat was pulled low over his eyes. His black coat was caked in dust. He rode slowly up the street with his men behind him. He stopped.

Kelly sat back in his saddle and slowly looked around him. His eyes stopped on Nash and Rock. He saw the Indian charm round Nash's neck. He looked down at Moss's leather bag and seemed to think for a moment. Then he turned to his men and spoke softly to them.

Two of the men turned their horses and went back down the street a little way. They stopped by the stable, got down and sat with their backs to the stable wall. The other two men rode on up the street past the saloon. They tied their horses to the rail and sat down outside. All four gunmen were watching Nash and Rock.

Kelly waited until his men were in place. Then he gave his own horse a kick. Kelly rode slowly up to the saloon, and stopped.

'Howdy,' he said. 'The name's Kid Kelly. People call me The Kid.' Rock stepped forward and stood beside Nash. His hand hung loose by his gun.

Kelly waited, then he said, 'You boys seen Moss?' 'Yeah,' said Nash softly. 'Then you know what I've come for,' said Kelly. 'Maybe,' said Nash.

'I've come for the map, boys,' said The Kid. 'If the map's in that bag, then I want it!' Nash slowly took the cigar from his mouth. He let it drop and crushed it into the dirt with his foot. 'So do we,' he said.

Rock stroked his gun-butt with his fingers. Kelly swung down from his horse. He lifted his hat and slowly wiped the sweat from his face. Then he turned to Nash.

'Mister, I guess you didn't hear me right,' he said. 'I want the bag with the map in, and I aim to get it.' 'Then you're gonna have to take it,' said Nash.

Kelly looked hard at Nash, then at Rock. 'You're dead men!' he growled. Then he pushed past them and went into the saloon.

Nash took a careful look at the four gun-men The Kid had brought with him. 'The man's got a point,' he said to Rock.

4

There were two chairs outside the saloon. Nash and Rock sat down in them. They stretched their legs, and leaned back. Nash looked down the street to his right. He could see two of Kid Kelly's men. They were sitting in the shade of the stable door. The other two men were further up the street to his left. They were sitting watching, waiting for Nash and Rock to make a move.

Nash figured that Kelly would not try anything in town. The Sheriff's office was just across the street from the saloon. It would be taking a chance to start anything with the law that close. Kelly would more likely wait until he and Rock left, and then ambush them somewhere on the trail.

'Hey Nash,' said Rock nodding towards the Kid's men. 'They're an ugly looking bunch.' 'So are you!' said Nash.

'Have you figured a way out yet?' asked Rock. 'Take it easy,' said Nash. 'Don't rush me.'

Before he could say any more there was a shout from down the street. Nash and Rock both turned to see what it was. A boy was running up the middle of the street. He was dirty and hot from running.

'The stage is coming, the stage is coming,' he yelled. The boy ran past Nash and Rock and up the steps of the stage office next to the saloon.

There was no sound for a moment. Then there was the soft rumble of the stage in the distance. The boy came out of the office and stood on the steps. Jed, the man who ran the stage office, came out with him. They both stood and looked down the street. A dog sleeping in the shade slowly opened one eye.

Suddenly six black horses dashed round the corner of the street. The clatter split the stillness of the town. The coach rolled from side to side. The big wheels crashed round. The dog jumped up and ran barking at the horses.

The driver pulled hard on the reins and the horses slowed down. The stage-coach rolled to a stop. 'Get away, get away!' yelled the driver at the dog. He tied up the reins and jumped down from his seat.

'OK, folks,' the driver said to the people in the coach. 'We're here to pick up the mail. You've got time to get something to eat. We move out in an hour.'

Rock watched the people get out of the stage. Then he turned to Nash and said 'OK then, partner, what are we going to do about Kelly?'

Nash thought for a long time, and then he said, 'We could make a run for it.' 'Too risky,' said Rock softly.

'We could try and shoot it out right here,' said Nash. 'Too messy,' said Rock.

'Or we could try the crazy way,' said Nash. Rock said nothing. 'See that stage?' said Nash. 'It takes the mail. Suppose we put the map in an envelope and mail it to the next town from here. That's Big Spring. Kid Kelly and his boys will never figure that the map is on the stage. So the stage goes right past them and takes the map out. We wait till night-fall and slip out of town past Kelly's men. We can collect the map at the stage office at Big Spring then get back to Sam.'

'You're right, Nash,' said Rock, 'that sure is the crazy way. So what if Kelly follows us and tries to attack us on the trail?'
'We can split up,' said Nash. 'One of us can lead Kelly and his men off on a false trail with Moss's bag. The other can go to Big Spring and collect the map.'

'Hmmm,' said Rock. 'And pardon me for asking, Nash, but which of us is going to be the sucker who leads The Kid and his men off on a false trail?' Nash smiled at him. 'Well,' he said, 'you're the man who's good with a gun. All you've got to do is give Kelly the slip and we'll meet up again at

Big Spring. So what do you say?' 'Nash, I've only got one thing to say,' said Rock. 'Bury me with my boots on.'

Nash laughed. Then he got up and walked along to the stage office. He took the map from the bag, put it in an envelope and sealed it. Jed was behind the counter in the office. Nash handed him the envelope and some money for the mail.

'I want it to go in the strong-box,' he said to Jed. 'It's OK, mister,' said Jed. 'The mail always goes in the strong-box.'

Nash went over to the door of the office and looked out. Kelly's men were talking amongst themselves. They did not seem to be looking. So he stepped out of the office into the street and walked slowly back to his chair.

At two o'clock the stage was ready to go. Jed came out of the stage office with the strong-box. It was heavy. As well as the mail there was some gold in the box.

'Look after this, Zak,' said Jed to the driver. 'There's a lot of money in here.' 'And a lot of map,' said Nash softly to Rock.

Zak lifted the strong-box onto the stage. He got up onto his seat. The guard with the shot-gun got up next to him.

Zak took hold of the reins. 'Go!' he yelled to the horses. 'Away! Away!'

The horses pulled away, the dog barked. The wheels turned, the boy waved. The stage picked up speed as it went down the street. It turned the corner and rolled off down the trail towards Big Spring.

5

The afternoon was hot. The sun burned in the sky. River Bend seemed to dry up in the heat. Nash and Rock sat in the shade outside the saloon. Rock dozed off. Nash watched the street.

Kid Kelly's men were still there. They had not moved. Just across the way the Sheriff came slowly out of his office. He sat down on a rocking chair by the door. He leaned back in the chair and pulled his hat over his eyes.

The town was still. The only sound was the piano in the saloon. It jangled away. The sound drifted softly along the street, fading away into the desert.

As the afternoon wore on the sun began to go down. Rock had been asleep for a couple of hours. Nash pushed his foot. Rock woke up. 'What's up?' he asked. 'Time to go and have a drink,' said Nash.

They went into the saloon. Kelly was sitting in the corner by the window. He was watching them. Nash asked for a bottle and two glasses. They stood at the bar and drank slowly. In the mirror behind the bar Rock could see The Kid watching them, with his eye on Moss's bag. After a few drinks Nash said, 'Let's play cards, if I still have some dollars left.'

They went over to the card table. Three men were playing. 'You got room for one more?' asked Nash. 'Sit down, boys,' said one of the men.

They played for about an hour. Kelly sat in the corner and watched them. Then Rock said, 'Here comes trouble.'

Nash looked up and saw Kelly cross the room. Rock's hand slid to his gun. Kelly came up to the table. 'Mind if I play?' he said, and sat down at the table. He looked across the table at Nash. It was a cold, hard stare. Nash looked back at The Kid.

'It's your deal,' said one of the other men at the table and handed the cards to Rock. Rock dealt the cards.

The game went fast. The heap of money in the middle of the table got bigger. Soon there were only two people left in the game — Nash and Kid Kelly.

Nash looked at the cards in his hand. Then he looked across at Kelly. Kelly smiled. 'I'll raise you five dollars,' said Nash. He pushed his five dollars into the middle of the table.

Kelly did not look at his cards. He just said, 'Here's your

five, and I'll raise you . . .' The Kid stopped for a moment. Then he said, 'I'll raise you twenty.'

He pushed the money into the middle of the table. Nash looked at his cards again. He looked at the money he had left. 'I've only got fifteen dollars,' he said to Kelly. 'I'm five short.'

Kelly looked at him. 'That's a pity, friend,' he said. 'But I'll tell you what. I like a good game of cards. So I'll forget about the other five in cash. That old bag you've got there,' said Kelly pointing at Moss's bag. 'That looks as if it's worth five dollars. Just put it on the table to cover your bet. It'll do instead of the money.'

Rock leaned over to Nash. Nash was looking at his cards. 'Don't do it, Nash, said Rock softly. 'If Kelly gets his hands on that bag he'll find out that the map has gone.' But Nash was thinking.

'What are you going to do, friend?' said Kelly. Nash looked at his cards, then at the bag, then at The Kid. Slowly he pushed the bag into the middle of the table. 'You're crazy,' said Rock, and put his hand over his eyes.

'OK, let's see what you've got,' said Nash. Kelly threw his cards down on the table. 'Full house, I win,' he said, and went to get the bag.

'Hold it, said Nash softly. 'You want to see my hand.' One by one he put the cards on the table. 'Four kings,' said Nash with a smile. 'I win.'

A mad look came into Kelly's eyes. 'No!' he yelled at Nash. 'You cheating dog!' He stood up and kicked his chair away. It skidded across the floor and crashed into the wall.

'I say you're a cheat, mister,' said The Kid. 'Now go for your gun!' 'He's too fast for you,' Rock said softly to Nash. 'Let me take him.' 'No,' said Nash. 'He'll kill you!' said Rock.

But Nash did not listen. He pushed his chair back and stood up slowly. The man at the piano stopped playing. The bar-tender got down behind the bar. There was a hush in the saloon. The only person who spoke was Nash.

'Nobody calls me a cheat!' he hissed. 'Then go for your gun, damn you!' yelled Kelly.

Nash backed slowly away from the table. He kept his eyes on Kelly. Kelly moved out from behind the table and stood with his back to the door. He looked hard at Nash.

'Come on! Draw!' said The Kid, and his hand dropped to his holster. Nash went for his gun, but Kelly was too fast for him. Kelly drew his gun first. 'He's got you!' yelled Rock.

Suddenly the door behind Kelly burst open and a man ran in. Kelly spun round to see what was happening. The man ran in between Kelly and Nash. It was Jed. 'The stage has been robbed! The stage has been robbed!' he shouted.

'Get out of the way!' yelled Kelly, and pushed him across the room. As Jed fell to one side Kelly fired at Nash, but he shot into thin air. Nash and Rock had gone, and so had the bag. The bullet ripped across the room and smashed into the mirror behind the bar. The mirror shattered into a thousand bits.

'What the hell is up with you, mister?' shouted Jed. But Kelly did not reply. He ran out through the swing doors into the street and shouted to his men.

Jed turned to the rest of the men in the saloon. 'The Sheriff found the passengers coming down the trail just outside of town,' he said. 'They're a bit shook up but they're OK. There was three men, shot the guard and got the strong-box. They busted it open, Zak says, and took the gold. The Sheriff wants you men for a posse. We're heading out after them bandits at dawn.'

6

Nash and Rock did not wait until dawn. They left River Bend by the light of the moon. If the bandits had got the gold from the strong-box they might have got the map as well. Nash and Rock had to move fast if they wanted to get it back.

The two cowboys rode hard. The moon was high and its soft light lit up the trail which led to Big Spring. They kept their eyes peeled for any sign of the stage. The horses galloped along between the tall cactus. Somewhere in the hills a wild dog cried to the moon.

The sun was just coming up when Nash and Rock reached the place where the stage had been robbed. The big coach lay on its side. One of the wheels had smashed against a rock by the side of the trail.

The dead guard lay on the ground by the coach. The wind softly blew his hair but his body was still. He was lying face down. One hand clawed the dirt of the ground. The other still clung to his shot-gun, a pale finger hooked around the trigger.

The horses had gone. The passengers had cut them loose and used them to get back to town. They had left their luggage. The bags and cases lay scattered around the coach.

Nash and Rock sat high on their horses and looked around them. A little way off from the coach lay the strong-box. The lid was open.

'There it is,' said Rock. 'Let's hope they left the mail alone and only took the gold,' said Nash.

They got down from their horses and walked over to the strong-box. The mail was still there. Nash bent down and flicked through the box. He smiled. 'Here it is,' said Nash. 'The map is still here.' He held up the envelope.

Nash looked up at Rock. Rock was standing very still, looking down the trail, 'Hey, Rock, it's here,' Nash said again. Rock still did not move. 'What's the matter?' asked Nash.

'Someone's coming,' said Rock. Nash listened. He could hear horses coming. They were coming fast. 'Come on,' said Rock. 'Let's get out of here.' Nash stuffed the map into Moss's bag and they both got onto their horses.

Suddenly five riders came around the bend back down the trail. 'Kelly!' yelled Nash. 'He must have followed us!' 'Move it!' said Rock.

Nash slapped his horse and the animal reared up on its hind legs. 'Hup!' shouted Nash, and he and Rock galloped away down the trail. There was the sound of shooting as Kelly opened fire behind them. 'Head up into the hills!' shouted Nash. 'We'll try and lose them up there.'

They turned and rode up into the hills above the trail. The sound of the horses' hooves rang out as they galloped between the huge rocks. They headed off up a narrow track which twisted away into the hills in front of them.

Kelly and his men galloped past the stage and turned up into the hills after Nash and Rock. The Kid was out in front with his gun drawn. His four men were behind him. Their horses raced wildly as they galloped up the slope.

Kelly's men fired again. Nash ducked as a hail of bullets spattered through the air over his head. Rock pulled out his gun, turned in the saddle and fired back.

Ahead of them the track twisted and turned deeper into the hills. The rocky cliffs on either side of the track seemed to be closing in on Nash and Rock. The track was getting narrower. As they galloped round a bend Nash suddenly yelled in panic. Ahead of them was a sheer cliff face, a solid wall of rock rising high above them. The track went no further. There was no way out.

'It's a dead end!' yelled Nash. 'They've got us trapped!'

7

There was no way out for Nash and Rock. Ahead of them was a sheer cliff face. Behind them came Kid Kelly and his men.

Nash pulled his horse up hard. The animal skidded to a halt on the loose stones. Nash jumped down and ran up into the rocks around the wall of the canyon. Rock stopped, grabbed his shot-gun and followed his partner.

As Kelly came up the track, Nash opened fire. He hit one of The Kid's men. The man fell forward from his horse and crashed to the ground. Kelly shouted to the rest of his men. They jumped down from their horses and scattered into the rocks on the other side of the canyon.

The blaze of gun-fire filled the canyon with a roar like thunder. The air was thick with lead. Rock swung his gun over the top of the rock he was crouching behind and pumped four quick shots at Kelly and his men. He ducked down as a shower of bullets came back. They smacked against the rock and whined through the air past his head. Nash re-loaded his gun, and started to fire again.

Then the shooting stopped. The sound of gun-fire died away between the cliffs. Nash took a quick look across the canyon. He could see nothing. Nobody moved. It was all very quiet.

The silence was broken by Kelly. 'We've got you boys holed up here!' he yelled. 'There's four of us and only two of you. If you want to shoot it out we're gonna kill you sooner or later. So why don't you just throw out the map, then we can all ride out of here peaceful. There's no use getting killed over a bit of paper, is there, boys?'

'The man is talking sense, Nash,' said Rock softly. 'He's also got us trapped,' said Nash, 'and he'll kill us even if we do give him the map.'

'So we shoot it out,' said Rock. 'Yeah,' said Nash. 'Now I'm going to work my way round the canyon to see if I can get a better shot at Kelly. You stay here.'

Rock nodded, and then he said, 'Nash . . . ' 'What?' asked Nash. 'Who's going to pay for the funeral?' said Rock. Nash smiled, and crawled off.

He moved slowly between the rocks until he found a place where he got a better view of The Kid and his men. All was quiet for a moment, then Kelly shouted again, 'Well what do you say, boys?' 'Kelly!' Nash yelled back. 'Go to hell!' And lifting up his gun he fired quickly across the canyon.

There was a cry from one of The Kid's men. He stood up holding his hands to his face. Blood was streaming between his fingers. He slumped onto the ground.

Kelly and his other two men opened fire. Chips of rock flew into the air as bullets slammed into the cliff behind Nash. He poked his gun over the top of the rock and fired back. Nash did not see one of the men start to edge his way around the canyon towards him.

Rock fired until his gun was empty, then bent down to re-load. He pushed the bullets quickly into the chamber. He opened the shot-gun he had with him. There were two rounds of buck-shot in the gun. He snapped the gun shut, then turned and slowly peered over the top of the rocks.

Nash was over to his right firing down into the canyon. Away from him and across the canyon Rock could see the flashes where Kelly and his men were firing back. But he could only see two men.

'Where's the other one?' thought Rock. He looked quickly around him. His eyes stopped on Nash. Nash had got down to re-load his gun. Something moved in the rocks behind Nash. It was Kid Kelly! He had worked his way round behind Nash. He had a gun aimed at Nash and Nash could not see him.

'Look out!' yelled Rock and stood up to shoot at Kelly. As he did so one of the men in the canyon fired and hit Rock in the arm. Rock swung round and blasted him with his shot-gun.

Nash looked up and saw The Kid above him. He was looking straight down the barrel of Kelly's gun. Nash's gun lay on the ground empty. Kelly smiled and squeezed the trigger.

Nash jerked to one side. As he did so, his hand went to the inside of his coat. He flicked out the knife and threw it hard at Kelly. The Kid's smile froze on his lips as the knife found his heart. He stood for a moment on the rocks above Nash. Then his body swayed slowly forward, hung for a moment in mid-air, then crashed down the cliff.

Nash wiped the sweat from his face. 'That was close,' he yelled to Rock. They both turned as they heard the sound of a horse. The last one of Kelly's men was galloping off down the canyon. He had given up.

Rock was holding his arm. 'I'm hit!' he said, as blood began to seep from under his fingers. 'Give me a hand, then let's get out of here.'

8

Sam was asleep in the sun. He sat and slept. His head rested on the back of his wheel-chair. His dog lay on the ground at his feet.

It was late afternoon. Smoke curled slowly from the chimney of the ranch house. There was a smell of cooking in the air. It was very still.

Slowly the dog opened one eye. He saw two men on horses far away. The men were coming towards the ranch. The dog could hear the horses galloping. The men were riding fast. They passed the gate and rode into the ranch. The dog stood up barking. Sam woke up.

The two men rode up to the front of the house. Sam picked up his gun. He pointed it at the two men. They looked dirty and tired. Then Sam smiled.

'Nash! Rock!' he said. 'Did you get it?' 'We got it,' said Nash and tossed the bag onto Sam's lap. 'It's in the bag,' said Rock.

Sam looked down at the bag and smiled. Then he said, 'Come on in, boys. You look hungry.' Nash and Rock got down from their horses. They all went into the house.

'Mary!' called Sam. 'Bring the whisky and some glasses.' A woman came in with the whisky. 'And there'll be two more for supper,' said Sam. Mary nodded and went out. She did not look at Nash or Rock.

Sam poured the drinks, then he picked up the bag. He opened it. He took out the gun, the watch and the silver dollars. Then he took out the other half of the map and laid it on the table. He put his own part of the map next to it and joined the two halves together. Now the map was all there.

Sam looked at it for a long time. At last he said, 'Moss hid the diamonds well.'

Nash filled his glass again. He drank the whisky. Then he said, 'You've got your map, Sam. Now let's have the money.'

Sam leaned back in his chair. 'How would you boys like to double your money? Turn that three hundred into six hundred dollars? Six hundred for each of you!'

Rock put his glass down. Nash took out a cigar. 'Keep talking,' said Rock. Nash struck a match on the table and lit his cigar. 'Yes, Sam,' he said. 'Tell us more.'

'Have a look at this map,' said Sam. He pushed the map

across to Nash. Nash looked hard at the map. He rolled the cigar between his teeth.

'It looks to me like those diamonds are hidden in pretty rocky country,' said Sam. 'I don't think I'll make it in this chair. It must be all of a week's ride to get there as well. How would you boys like to go and get the diamonds for me? I'll give you six hundred dollars each for the job.'

Nash pushed the map away. He took the cigar out of his mouth and blew out the smoke. 'No,' he said.

'Come on, boys,' said Sam. 'Six hundred dollars to go and dig up a few diamonds!'

'Sam baby,' said Nash. 'A few diamonds is a lot of money. We'll go and dig them up, but we split them three ways. We split the diamonds between you, me and Rock, or we have no deal.'

Sam looked at Nash for a moment. Then he picked the map up. 'OK,' he said to Nash and Rock. 'You get the diamonds and we split them three ways. Now let's eat.' He turned to the kitchen and yelled, 'Mary! Where's the supper?'

Two hours later Nash and Rock had washed and eaten. The sun had begun to go down. The three men were talking in front of the house. Two fresh horses stood waiting. There was a pick and a shovel tied to the saddle of one horse. The other had a sack of food slung over it.

'Why don't you boys wait till tomorrow?' asked Sam. 'No,' said Nash. 'The sooner we go, the sooner we get to the diamonds. We'll ride for a few hours tonight and then make camp.' 'OK,' said Sam.

'If it's going to take a week to get there,' said Rock, 'every hour counts.' He got onto his horse. Nash jumped up on the other horse.

'Good luck, boys,' said Sam. 'I hope you make it.' 'We'll make it,' said Nash. 'Keep a bottle of whisky and two glasses ready for us. We'll be back in two weeks with the diamonds.'

'So long,' said Rock. 'I'll be seeing you,' said Sam.

Nash and Rock turned their horses and galloped off down the track. Sam waved and watched them go. He waited until they were out of sight, then he went inside.

9

After a mile or two Nash slowed his horse down. Rock came up beside him. They talked as they rode.

'I've been thinking,' said Nash. 'Oh, no,' said Rock. 'Do you know what's better than a three-way split?' asked Nash.

Rock looked across at him. 'No, Nash,' he said. 'What is better than a three-way split?' 'A two-way split,' said Nash.

'A two-way split?' said Rock. 'That's right,' said Nash. 'A two-way split.' Rock thought for a moment, and then he smiled.

'You mean that when we find the diamonds we keep them?' 'That's right,' said Nash. 'And we don't split them with Sam?' asked Rock. 'No,' said Nash.

Rock laughed. 'That's a good idea, Nash,' he said. 'A very good idea. But what about Sam? What do you think he'll do when he finds out?' 'What can he do?' said Nash. 'He's stuck in that wheel-chair.'

'Hey, Nash,' said Rock. 'We're rich! Wait till we get to

Kansas City with all that money!' 'Just think of all that whisky! And all those pretty girls!' said Nash. 'And all those pretty girls! And all that whisky!' said Rock. 'So let's go and get the diamonds!' said Nash. 'Kansas City here we come.'

He slapped his horse with his hand. The horse galloped off down the track. Rock galloped after him. The sun was just setting as they went over the hill. The cloud of dust behind them blew softly in the wind.

10

Meanwhile, back at the ranch, Sam was sitting at the table. He had watched Nash and Rock ride off. Now he lit the lamp.

Sam picked up the old leather bag that Moss had sent the map in. He put it on the table and got out his knife. Slowly he cut into the bottom of the bag. The leather split, showing a secret pocket with something hidden inside.

Sam lifted the bag. He shook it gently. Out fell a glittering mass . . . it was the diamonds!

Sam smiled. Then he laughed. 'A three-way split?' he said, and laughed till the tears ran down his face. 'Oh, boys,' he said softly to himself. 'You won't see me in two weeks. I'll be long gone. You'll never see me or the diamonds again!'

Then he turned in his chair. 'Mary!' he yelled into the kitchen. 'Go and pack some things. We're leaving first thing in the morning. We're going to Kansas City. They'll never find us there!'

A complete list of Spirals

Stories

Jim Alderson
Crash in the Jungle
The Witch Princess

Jan Carew
Death Comes to the Circus

Susan Duberley
The Ring

**Keith Fletcher and
Susan Duberley**
Nightmare Lake

John Goodwin
Dead-end Job

Paul Groves
Not that I'm Work-shy
The Third Climber

Anita Jackson
The Actor
The Austin Seven
Bennet Manor
Dreams
The Ear
A Game of Life or Death
No Rent to Pay

Paul Jennings
Eye of Evil
Maggot

Margaret Loxton
The Dark Shadow

Patrick Nobes
Ghost Writer

Kevin Philbin
Summer of the Werewolf

John Townsend
Beware the Morris Minor
Fame and Fortune
SOS

David Walke
Dollars in the Dust

Plays

Jan Carew
Computer Killer
No Entry
Time Loop

John Godfrey
When I Count to Three

Nigel Gray
An Earwig in the Ear

Paul Groves
Tell Me Where it Hurts

Barbara Mitchelhill
Punchlines
The Ramsbottoms at Home

Madeline Sotheby
Hard Time at Batwing Hall

John Townsend
Cheer and Groan
The End of the Line
Hanging by a Fred
The Lighthouse Keeper's Secret
Making a Splash
Murder at Muckleby Manor
Over and Out
Rocking the Boat
Taking the Plunge

David Walke
The Bungle Gang Strike Again
The Good, the Bad and the Bungle
Package Holiday